THE PASTEL MAGIC BOOK OF
TAROT SPREADS

DIVINING AND JOURNALING YOUR WAY TO YOUR HIGHER SELF

Maria Morales

Copyright © 2019 Maria Morales

All rights reserved.

ISBN: 9781793942791

DEDICATION

To everyone who ever encouraged me to say "Why not?"

CONTENTS

	Acknowledgments	i
1	Introduction	1
2	How to Use this Book	3
3	Inviting Positivity	6
4	Calming Breath	10
5	Time May Change Us	14
6	Yes, Queen!	18
7	Dream Big	22
8	I am Beauty	26
9	Level Up	30
10	Moving Forward	34
11	Breathe In, Breathe Out	38
12	I am Love	42
13	I am Life	46
14	Making Happiness	50
15	Popping Bottles	54
16	Pick Me Up	58
17	Draw the Line	62
18	Lavender Fields	66
19	Building Bridges	70
20	Attract your Pack	74

21	Just Focus	78
22	I am Empowered	82
23	Autumn Renewal	86
24	Spring Rebirth	90
25	Lunar Cycles	94
26	Healing	98
27	Dealing with Rejection	102
28	Truest You	106
29	Love Letter	110
30	Crystal Clarity	114
31	Trailblazing	118
32	I am Strong	122

ACKNOWLEDGMENTS

This book would not exist without so many people who made me realize what I could do with what I have. I would like to thank Eddie, for always supporting my ideas, Veronica, for being a source of positivity from the moment I met her, Nikki, for being a source of inspiration and encouragement, Ariana, for showing me how to always strive to be a better person, and my parents, for feeding my ego a little too much when I was a kid.

INTRODUCTION

Tarot spreads allow you to contemplate a given theme by asking questions related to that theme and guiding you to the answer through tarot cards. This hybrid book of spreads/journal is meant to encourage you to explore themes centered around personal development and becoming the best version of yourself. Introspect and reflect with guided questions and quick discussions that lead you to the path of positivity.

Journaling is the second function of this book. It may not seem like much at the time, but writing in a journal is a precious gift to your present and future self. It allows you to acknowledge what you feel and what matters to you in a given moment. It allows you to think about and better understand your own thought process and emotional response. Capturing even the most mundane moments gives you the chance to travel back through time and relive your day-to-day and see how your way of thinking and reacting has grown.

The best way to journal is by making it a regular habit. But where to begin? It can be difficult to sit down with a pen and blank notebook and channel insight and wit on command every day. That's what this book is for. It's a starting point and an exercise in tapping into a mindful state to record all the wonderful ideas and feelings and nuances floating in your mind, waiting to be immortalized. It will prompt you when you don't know what else to write about, and eventually, you just might find yourself growing as a writer and thinker, more aware of ideas to put to paper.

HOW TO USE THIS BOOK

Honestly? However you want. Do a spread a day, in order. Sporadically skim through until one calls to you. Do it alone or form an entire coven and meet under the light of the full moon every month. Stick to short answers or get a blank notebook and use the questions as a starting point for an in-depth writing prompt. Don't write anything down at all and just meditate! Cover the pages in lamination sheets and make a reusable wet-erase book. Who cares how you use this book? As long as you do it in a way that's fulfilling for you, nothing else matters.

That being said, here are some actual instructions:

- ✧ If you don't have a tarot or oracle deck yet, find one that speaks to you. I hear the Pastel Magic Tarot is pretty cute.
- ✧ Find a guide that you understand. Make sure the guide matches the type of deck you have. Most tarot decks these days follow the Rider Waite Smith format, and there are many, many guides for it, including free guides available online or as apps.
- ✧ After shuffling, focusing on your questions, and doing whatever else is a part of your personal reading ritual (cleansing, meditating, etc.), draw your cards. The order they are drawn in will correspond to the numbered questions.

- ✧ Consult your guide to determine what the card means in the context of the question. For practiced and intuitive readers, this is optional but encouraged.
- ✧ If you pull a "negative" card for a question that should have positive answers, don't panic. Some things aren't always what they seem at face value. This is your cue to channel your inner PR agent and spin that card as something positive. Think of it as a challenge round or an opportunity to address your shadows.
- ✧ Use the short response sections to write what you think the card means. If the given spaces aren't enough, that's okay. This is just a starting point for you. Feel free to keep an accompanying notebook or even try recording your thoughts out loud.
- ✧ Use the free response section to write down how the card meanings relate to your life, any patterns you notice, and how the cards relate to each other.
- ✧ Go back every so often to see if you feel the same about a spread as you did when you wrote it. **Enjoy the memories you make.**

THE SPREADS

INVITING POSITIVITY

  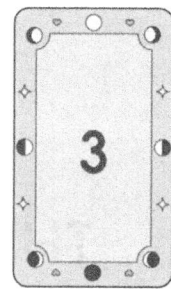

It's easy to look around and see what other people have and what's going on in other lives and feel like we're somehow lacking. Instead of comparing and envying, focus on the good in your own life. By taking a moment to appreciate what you have, your attitude will shift towards one of gratitude, opening you up to receive positivity.

1. WHAT DO I HAVE TO BE EXCITED ABOUT?

2. WHAT DO I HAVE TO BE GRATEFUL FOR?

3. WHAT AM I READY TO RECEIVE?

FREE RESPONSE

CALMING BREATH

Emotions and situations can get overwhelming. When it feels like things are too much to handle, it helps to stop and take a deep breath before taking action in a calmer state of mind. To help reach that state of mind, you can take a moment to focus on one detail instead of the entire situation. Taking one thing at a time can make a big problem seem less intimidating by breaking it down into a series of smaller ones, but you might need a little guidance on where to start. From there, you can start thinking about how to steady the situation and how to maintain your cool. With practice and mindfulness, it gets easier to react calmly and productively to things that used to push you past your limit. Don't forget—it's normal to have strong emotional reactions. It's healthy to let yourself feel what you need to feel to process something. But whenever you're ready, go ahead and take a nice, deep, calming breath.

1. WHAT CAN I FOCUS ON?

_____
_____
_____
_____
_____
_____
_____

2. WHAT CAN I DO TO STABILIZE THE SITUATION?

_____
_____
_____
_____
_____
_____
_____

3. HOW CAN I STAY CALM AND COLLECTED?

_____
_____
_____
_____
_____
_____
_____

FREE RESPONSE

TIME MAY CHANGE US

When someone we love starts to change and grow, it can inspire us or it can bring out envy, jealousy, and fear of being left behind. If someone close to us starts to change for the better, it can leave us wondering if we're good enough and if we need to change, too. This can be an uncomfortable feeling, which many of us want to avoid. This can manifest in negative, hurtful ways as we attempt to hold back our loved one through criticisms and discouraging words. Instead of trying to hold them back, ask yourself how you can be supportive and happy for this positive change. Ask yourself how you can make this an opportunity for your own development and learn to grow *together*.

1. WHAT AM I AFRAID OF LOSING?

_____
_____
_____

2. WHERE AM I HOLDING BACK MY OWN GROWTH?

_____
_____
_____

3. HOW CAN I BE SUPPORTIVE?

_____
_____
_____

4. HOW CAN I STIMULATE MY OWN GROWTH?

_____
_____
_____

5. HOW CAN WE MOVE FORWARD TOGETHER?

_____
_____
_____

FREE RESPONSE

YES, QUEEN!

Sometimes it's easy to feel common and a little ordinary. This feeling couldn't be further from the truth. We all have a little majesty to us—every individual is unique, special, and proof the world is incredible. Every so often we need to remember that to appreciate who we are. This can come from internal positivity and it can come from loving people who bolster each other and lift each other to new heights. When everyone is confident in themselves, we can accomplish great things, so hold your crown high, because you are royally gifted (and yes, *anyone* can channel their inner queen, regardless of gender)!

1. HOW CAN I CHANNEL MY MAJESTY?

2. HOW CAN I BOOST MY CONFIDENCE?

3. HOW CAN I ENCOURAGE THOSE AROUND ME?

FREE RESPONSE

DREAM BIG

Many of us have been taught that if we can dream something, we can make it a reality, so why not dream as big as possible? If you're going to set your mind to something, why not challenge yourself and set things one step further? Even if you don't always reach your goals 100% of the time, reaching beyond the bare minimum will get you farther and farther every time.

1. HOW CAN I EXPAND ON MY GOALS?

_____
_____
_____
_____
_____
_____
_____

2. HOW CAN I BE MORE AMBITIOUS?

_____
_____
_____
_____
_____
_____
_____

3. HOW CAN I WORK TOWARD MY GOALS?

_____
_____
_____
_____
_____
_____
_____

FREE RESPONSE

I AM BEAUTY

There are some days we look in the mirror and just don't like what we see. Sometimes we take a look at ourselves and don't like who we are. This is *no* way to get in touch with our highest selves. We must embrace who we are in spirit and love the vessel carrying that spirit. This doesn't mean we have to believe we are perfect, but it does mean loving the little flaws that represent our humanity. It's these little details that make us interesting. This can be a challenge for some people, because loving yourself is hard work! We see our reflections and pictures all the time and we get used to the image. We fixate on the imperfections that no one else is even noticing. What we need is to focus on the beautiful qualities that make us unique and to try and see ourselves through the eyes of those who love us. Maybe this way we can learn how to love ourselves.

1. WHAT IS A BEAUTIFUL QUALITY ABOUT ME?

_____
_____
_____
_____
_____
_____
_____

2. HOW CAN I SEE MY BEAUTY MORE CLEARLY?

_____
_____
_____
_____
_____
_____
_____

3. HOW CAN I APPRECIATE MYSELF MORE?

_____
_____
_____
_____
_____
_____
_____

FREE RESPONSE

LEVEL UP

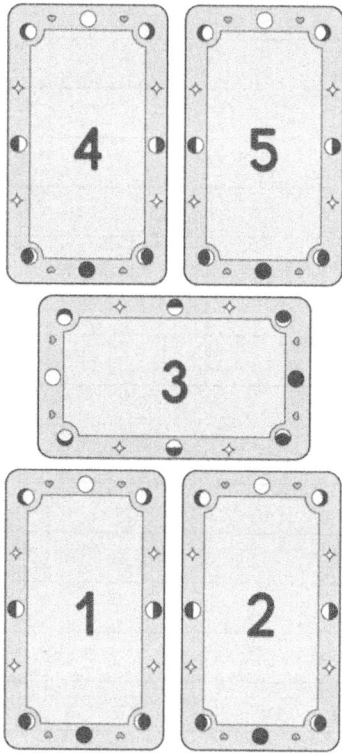

When we don't challenge ourselves, we stagnate. We lose momentum. It's important to try to gain new skills and hone the ones we have because it stimulates us and drives us to accomplish things we couldn't do before. Think about something you could be better at and then do what it takes to *become better.* Start small and make gradual improvements. In time, you'll be amazed by how far you've come.

1. WHAT SKILL CAN I WORK ON DEVELOPING?

_____
_____
_____

2. HOW CAN I DEVELOP IT FURTHER?

_____
_____
_____

3. WHAT CHALLENGES MIGHT I FACE?

_____
_____
_____

4. HOW CAN I OVERCOME THESE OBSTACLES?

_____
_____
_____

5. WHAT DO I HAVE TO GAIN?

_____
_____
_____

FREE RESPONSE

MOVING FORWARD

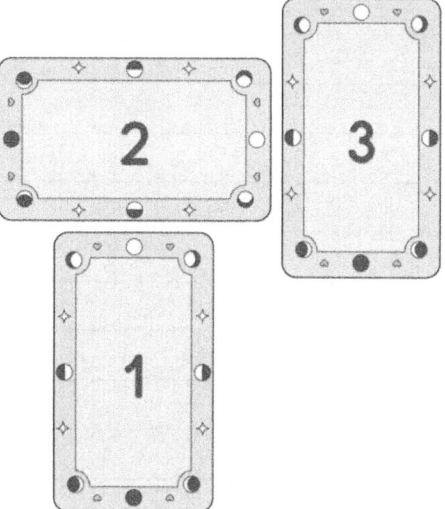

Sometimes moving forward is easy. Other times we can't seem to gather the momentum we need to get started. Take some time to make sure you understand what could be holding you back and how to free yourself from it. At that point, get ready to move ahead. Remember, not everything that is good for us at one point will *always* be good for us. We need to make sure that we're not burdening ourselves unnecessarily if we want to push ourselves as far as we can. Let go of the things that no longer serve you. It'll free you up to take on things you do need on your journey.

1. WHAT IS HOLDING ME BACK?

_____
_____
_____
_____
_____
_____
_____

2. HOW CAN I RELEASE WHAT NO LONGER SERVES ME?

_____
_____
_____
_____
_____
_____
_____

3. HOW CAN I TAKE MY FIRST STEPS FORWARD?

_____
_____
_____
_____
_____
_____
_____

FREE RESPONSE

BREATHE IN, BREATHE OUT

Take a deep breath. Inhale through the nose, and exhale through the mouth. Take another breath and this time, visualize yourself drawing in positivity. Imagine you are expelling negativity and transforming it into positive energy. Do this any time you feel like you are being bogged down and need to cleanse yourself.

1. HOW CAN I ATTRACT MORE POSITIVITY?

2. HOW CAN I BANISH NEGATIVITY?

3. HOW CAN I RADIATE POSITIVE ENERGY?

FREE RESPONSE

I AM LOVE

Love is a powerful, beautiful force. It can inspire us to do incredible things and gives us the strength to become the best versions of ourselves. In order to grow, we must open ourselves up to receive the love being offered to us, and in turn, offer our love to those we wish to see succeed in life. This can be more challenging than it sounds. Sometimes it's difficult to accept love if we feel undeserving of it. This means we need to love ourselves more. Sometimes it can be difficult to express love because it makes us vulnerable. This means we need to trust more.

1. HOW CAN I EXPRESS MY LOVE?

_____
_____
_____
_____
_____
_____
_____

2. HOW CAN I BE BETTER AT ACCEPTING LOVE?

_____
_____
_____
_____
_____
_____
_____

3. HOW CAN I LOVE MYSELF MORE?

_____
_____
_____
_____
_____
_____
_____

FREE RESPONSE

I AM LIFE

    Routine is great for us in some ways. Regular sleep patterns are healthy, and having a repeatable schedule allows us to relax and feel safe and settled in a predictable pattern. Routine can also, let's face it, be incredibly boring day-in and day-out. Yes, it makes life easy, but spontaneity makes life worth living! This doesn't mean you have to throw your whole routine out the window and get on the next plane to another continent. Any moment can become something new if you learn how to shift your perspective and look at it in a different way. Take some time to think about how you can make your regular day a little richer. If you have a cup of coffee every morning, learn about where your coffee comes from and how it's made. If you have to go to the bank, think about all the other people from different walks of life who have run the same errand. A fresh eye can take little moments and make them feel like big adventures.

1. WHAT CAN I DO TO FEEL ALIVE?

2. HOW CAN I ADD EXCITEMENT TO MY LIFE?

3. HOW CAN I APPRECIATE THE LITTLE THINGS MORE?

FREE RESPONSE

MAKING HAPPINESS

Everyone has bad days. Sometimes those days can stretch into weeks or even years and it can be draining, disheartening, and outright miserable. If we could just make up our minds to be happy and *be* happy, no one would ever be depressed, but obviously it's not that easy. Emotional health is a deeply complex thing and saying that we can just choose happiness greatly disparages those who live with depression. We can, however, sometimes find little ways to improve our mood and if that opportunity is in our grasp, it is so important that we take it. This tarot spread will not cure depression. It will, however, give you a little guidance in those moments that you're feeling a bit down and have the energy to push yourself towards happiness and just need that initial nudge. If you do deal with depression, please reach out. Help is always here for you.

1. HOW CAN I ELEVATE MY MOOD?

_____
_____
_____
_____
_____
_____
_____

2. WHAT CAN I DO TO FEEL BETTER WHEN I'M UPSET?

_____
_____
_____
_____
_____
_____
_____

3. HOW CAN I SPREAD JOY?

_____
_____
_____
_____
_____
_____
_____

FREE RESPONSE

POPPING BOTTLES

Talking about emotions can be a difficult, awkward thing with which many of us struggle. Often, it's easier to just keep things to ourselves, closed off from others. The problem is that when we keep things bottled up, pressure tends to build over time, and small problems can grow and erupt as major outbursts. We need to take the time to open up about things and let out our emotions in a healthy way. Like opening a champagne bottle, we need to be aware of how we're unbottling. You wouldn't point a champagne cork at someone, so you shouldn't aim to harm anyone with your emotions either. Find an appropriate way to let out the things you've been holding in, and then celebrate the relief.

1. WHAT HAVE I BEEN KEEPING BOTTLED UP?

_____
_____
_____
_____
_____
_____

2. HOW CAN I RELEASE?

_____
_____
_____
_____
_____
_____

3. HOW CAN I CELEBRATE LETTING IT OUT?

_____
_____
_____
_____
_____
_____

FREE RESPONSE

PICK ME UP

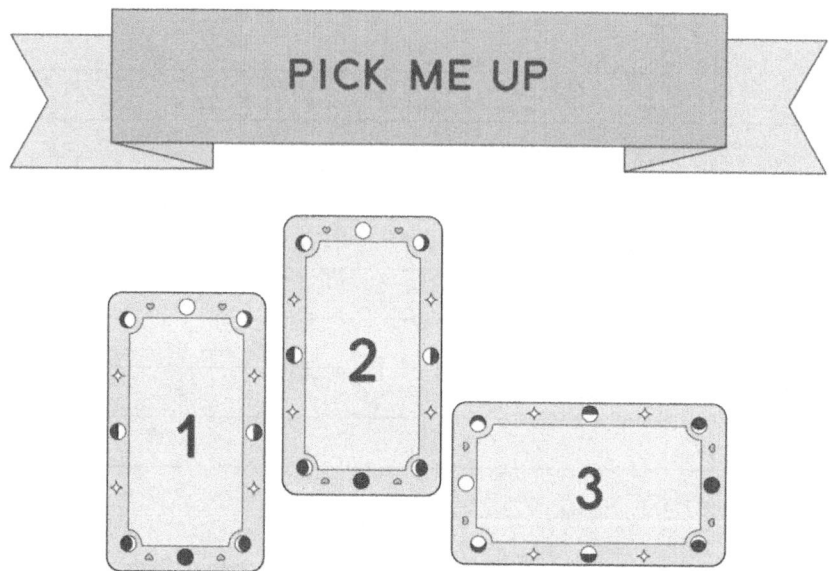

By midafternoon, many of us are dragging ourselves to the coffee pot, desperately in need of a caffeine "pick-me-up" to get us through the rest of the day. When working towards our goals, we can feel a similar sort of burnout. What we need is something to keep that spark alive and get us moving again. And don't forget—sometimes a break is more effective than a caffeine boost.

1. WHAT DO I NEED TO GET DONE?

2. WHAT CAN I DO TO MOTIVATE MYSELF?

3. HOW CAN I PICK MYSELF UP WHEN I LOSE MOTIVATION?

FREE RESPONSE

DRAW THE LINE

It can be difficult to say no, especially if you try to make everyone happy. Unfortunately, saying yes to everyone else can mean saying no to yourself and your own wants and needs. There's a misconception that it's selfish to put your needs before others' but the truth is you can't expect to make anyone else happy when your own needs aren't being met. Taking care of yourself puts you in a stronger, healthier position to help others, so drawing boundaries is an important skill for people who help people. It isn't easy, but with practice and guidance, it can become integrated in who you are and will get easier over time.

1. WHERE DO I NEED TO SET BOUNDARIES?

_____
_____
_____
_____
_____

2. HOW CAN I ESTABLISH THOSE BOUNDARIES?

_____
_____
_____
_____
_____

3. HOW CAN I ENFORCE THOSE BOUNDARIES?

_____
_____
_____
_____
_____

4. WHAT DO I HAVE TO GAIN FROM SETTING BOUNDARIES?

_____
_____
_____
_____
_____

FREE RESPONSE

LAVENDER FIELDS

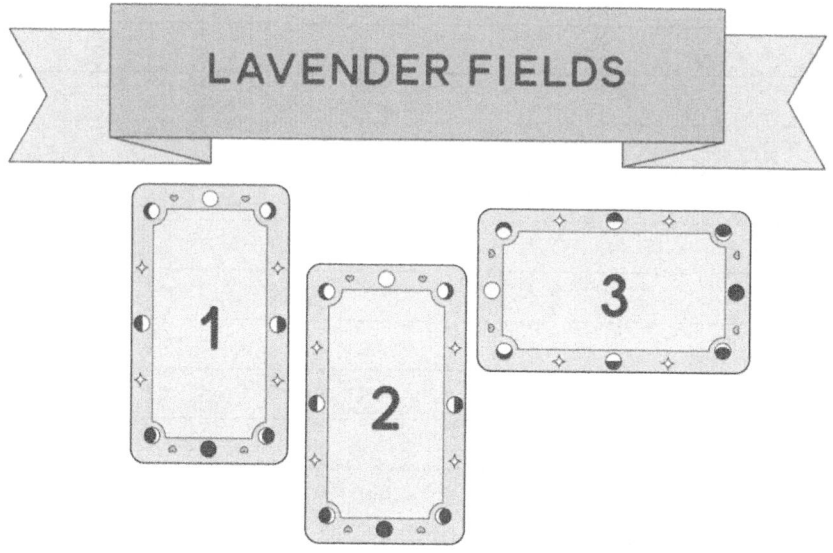

Imagine sitting on a porch, looking out at acres of lavender, while the calming scent wafts towards you on a gentle breeze. Maybe you're not a big fan of lavender. Maybe you prefer luxuriating in a bubble bath, glass of rosé in hand. Or perhaps a bottle of ice cold beer on the couch is more your speed. Whatever it is, we all have some idea or image that calms us, but sometimes we get so stressed that we forget how to switch gears and slow down to relax. Take a moment to consider whether anything is causing you stress, then think about how you can let those stresses go, at least long enough to indulge in a quiet, relaxing moment.

1. WHAT IS CAUSING ME STRESS?

_____
_____
_____
_____
_____
_____
_____

2. HOW CAN I DE-STRESS?

_____
_____
_____
_____
_____
_____
_____

3. HOW CAN I INDULGE IN RELAXATION?

_____
_____
_____
_____
_____
_____
_____

FREE RESPONSE

BUILDING BRIDGES

Feeling isolated and disconnected from others is common, but that doesn't make it any less difficult. When we feel like we're on our own, our burdens are heavier, our obstacles more challenging. We can be independent and self-sufficient, but we need to connect to other people once in a while to share in our triumphs and to support us in our low points. It is all important to remember to reach out from time to time, to nurture a support system, and to be a part of someone else's support system. When you feel like you're on your own, stop and consider how things might be different if you let yourself be a part of something bigger. More often than not, the change would be a positive one.

1. WHERE AM I DISCONNECTED FROM OTHERS?

2. HOW CAN I BRIDGE THAT GAP?

3. WHAT WILL COME FROM THIS CONNECTION?

FREE RESPONSE

ATTRACT YOUR PACK

In a way, every individual represents the combination of influences in their life. We are shaped by our experiences and by the way we interact with others. It makes sense, then, to surround ourselves with positive influences who inspire us to make the most of our lives and be the best people we can be. We should find people who resonate with us, who understand us, and who elevate us. This can be challenging, especially in small communities, but with the internet, social media, and meetup apps, it's easier than ever to find the people with whom we can form a special bond. We cannot be passive about this. We must actively seek out the type of people we want in our lives or we must make it known that we are open to meeting people who want to grow with us. These relationships are the ones that outlast those formed out of convenience, so remember that they may take more effort to find, but ultimately they are worth it.

1. HOW CAN I ATTRACT PEOPLE WHO RESONATE WITH ME?

_____
_____
_____
_____
_____
_____
_____

2. HOW CAN I ELEVATE OTHERS?

_____
_____
_____
_____
_____
_____
_____

3. HOW CAN I BOND WITH OTHERS?

_____
_____
_____
_____
_____
_____
_____

FREE RESPONSE

JUST FOCUS

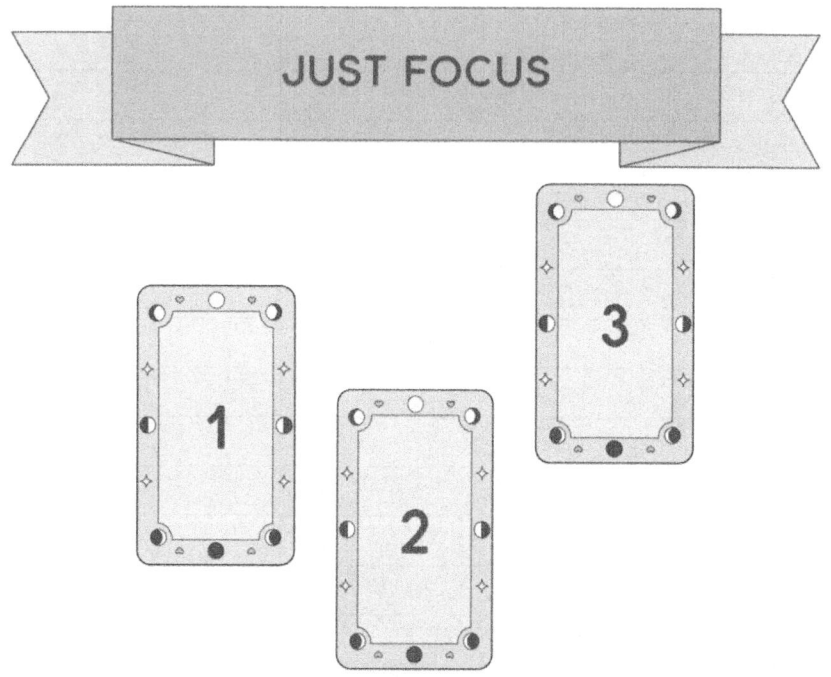

We live in a world full of distractions. So much information, recreation, and enrichment is available on our phones alone, not to mention what's waiting for us just outside our doorsteps. This is generally a wonderful thing, but when we need to get one specific thing done, it can feel like we're being taunted by all the things we *could* be doing instead. While it's important to take breaks and make sure we're not too absorbed in our work, we have to be careful not to take things too far in the other direction. Find a way that's effective for you to tune out the distractions and buckle down to get your task done. You have so much to offer the world. Don't let distractions keep you from making your contribution.

1. WHAT DO I NEED TO GET DONE?

_____
_____
_____
_____
_____
_____

2. WHAT IS DISTRACTING ME?

_____
_____
_____
_____
_____
_____

3. HOW CAN I GET BACK ON TRACK?

_____
_____
_____
_____
_____
_____

FREE RESPONSE

I AM EMPOWERED

We are all relatively small in the scale of the universe. Sometimes we're overly aware of how small that is and it can be overwhelming to think we're competing with infinity for significance. The thing is, we don't need to compete with infinity. Within our circles, however big or small they are, we have significance. We just need to remember that and know that we can make huge waves if we're confident enough in our own abilities. That's why it's important to take time to think powerfully and recognize the might of our imagination and determination. The best part is, you can lead by example and inspire others to unlock their power potential, and they in turn can make the effect grow exponentially. Know how expansive your influence is and start a chain reaction.

1. HOW CAN I MAKE MY THOUGHTS MORE POWERFUL?

_____
_____
_____
_____

2. HOW CAN I TURN THOUGHTS INTO ACTIONS?

_____
_____
_____
_____

3. WHAT CAN I ACCOMPLISH?

_____
_____
_____
_____

4. HOW CAN I EMPOWER OTHERS?

_____
_____
_____
_____

FREE RESPONSE

AUTUMN RENEWAL

Every year, the earth goes through its seasonal life cycle. As we go into autumn, plants start to prepare for the dormancy of winter by diverting nutrients to their roots and animals prepare by stocking up on food or fattening up for hibernation. This preparation and prioritization enables them to get through the harshness of winter. In the same way, we should recognize what things are not a priority, and where we need to rest in order to make it through a challenging time. This doesn't necessarily mean we're cutting things out for good, it just means cutting down on certain things to divert our energy somewhere more critical until winter is over.

1. WHAT IN MY LIFE NEEDS A BREAK?

_____
_____
_____
_____
_____
_____
_____

2. IN WHAT WAYS CAN I REST?

_____
_____
_____
_____
_____
_____
_____

3. IN WHAT WAYS CAN I PREPARE?

_____
_____
_____
_____
_____
_____
_____

FREE RESPONSE

SPRING REBIRTH

Whether we mean to or not, we tend to mimic the seasons of the earth. Things that are part of our day to day life change as time goes on and it's normal for things to phase out of our normal routine. It's also normal to want to reawaken some parts of ourselves or old habits that we've let fall dormant. Think about good things that were once a part of your life that would benefit you if they were reintroduced. Think about some old habits that you're better off without and what new things you can try in their place. Like the earth taking winter as an opportunity to prepare for a beautiful spring, you can take these moments to consider where you have room for growth and regrowth.

1. WHAT IN MY LIFE HAS BEEN DORMANT?

_____
_____
_____
_____
_____
_____
_____

2. WHAT IS REAWAKENING?

_____
_____
_____
_____
_____
_____
_____

3. WHAT NEW THINGS ARE GROWING?

_____
_____
_____
_____
_____
_____
_____

FREE RESPONSE

LUNAR CYCLES

There is something wild and magical about observing the cycles of the moon. When we watch it wax and wane we can feel it tug and release its hold on us like the ebb and flow of the tides. Think of the forces in your life like the cycles of the moon. Observe the forces that grow stronger and the things in your life that release their hold on you. When you feel something has its strongest influence on you, consider that your full moon and prepare for it to start letting go.

1. WHAT IS WANING OR LEAVING?

___

2. WHAT IS IN FULL EFFECT?

___

3. WHAT IS GROWING IN STRENGTH?

___

FREE RESPONSE

HEALING

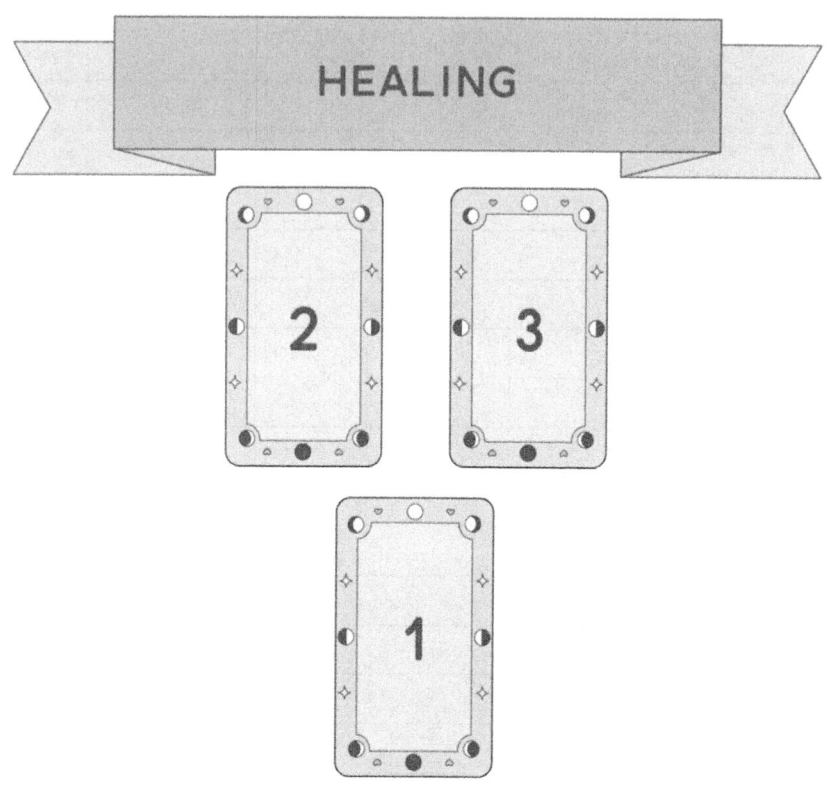

If only we could all go through life pain-free. Alas, everyone gets hurt at one point or another, but we can take solace in the fact that every pain is something that can teach us or that can make us stronger. The important thing is to avoid lashing out in pain, and to hold on to who you are at your best, even when you feel like you're at your worst. One of the most important skills any of us can learn is to know how to treat ourselves when we are hurt. Think about the things that help you feel strong again, that comfort you and reassure you. Taking care of yourself when you are hurt will help you heal stronger and knowing that will help you each time you go through the experience. In time, your confidence in your ability to heal will make each pain a little easier to overcome.

1. HOW CAN I RECONNECT WITH MYSELF?

2. HOW CAN I DRESS MY WOUNDS?

3. HOW CAN I MAKE SURE I WILL HEAL?

FREE RESPONSE

DEALING WITH REJECTION

We are all incredible beings, but that doesn't mean everyone else will always recognize it. Inevitably, we all find ourselves facing rejection and it can be challenging to stay positive in these circumstances. Fortunately, it just takes the right perspective to remember that every rejection is actually an opportunity for something else that we're not seeing yet. Each time we are denied for one thing, that means we are open to try many other things. There's no need to be bitter or angry about rejection (but maybe it's okay to indulge in those reactions for a moment). The important thing is to move on and reframe the situation in a positive light.

1. WHY IS THIS REJECTION ACTUALLY A GOOD THING?

_____
_____
_____
_____
_____
_____
_____

2. HOW IS THIS A NEW OPPORTUNITY?

_____
_____
_____
_____
_____
_____
_____

3. HOW DO I MOVE ON?

_____
_____
_____
_____
_____
_____
_____

FREE RESPONSE

TRUEST YOU

Some say that every person presents a different face to everyone they know. It makes sense. Who you are with your closest friends may not be the person you want to be around your boss. It's natural to shift and tailor our presentation to the audience, but sometimes it can feel overwhelming and like we're losing track of who we really are. Every so often, it's a good idea to pause and reflect on who you are on your own, with no one watching. Think about the things you hide from others and why you feel the need to hide them. Think about whether you've been too preoccupied with the image you present to know if it's actually true to you. Try to live honestly and you can get to know who you truly are.

1. IN WHAT WAY AM I NOT LIVING MY TRUTH?

_____
_____
_____
_____
_____
_____

2. HOW CAN I LIVE MORE TRUTHFULLY?

_____
_____
_____
_____
_____
_____

3. HOW CAN I EMBRACE WHO I AM?

_____
_____
_____
_____
_____
_____

FREE RESPONSE

LOVE LETTER

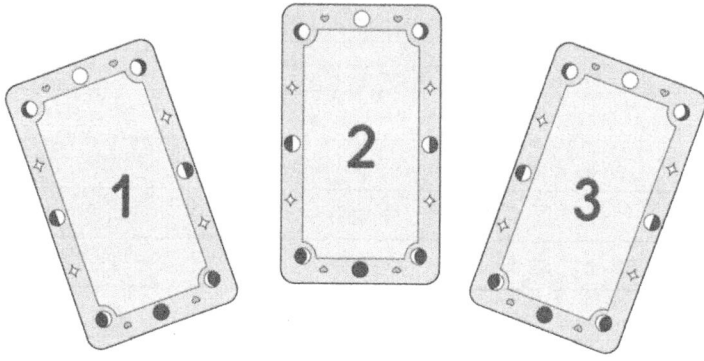

It's so easy to think about someone we love and list the many things we love about them. For some reason it's a little more challenging to extend that same kind of love to ourselves. It's a good exercise to, every so often, think about ourselves the way we think about our loved ones. If we could see ourselves from a third person perspective, what are the things we would admire? What are the things we would find endearing if we saw them in someone else? A fun way to think of it is a love letter. If you received a love letter, what are the things you would hope to see in it? This is your opportunity to get that perfect love letter. Write one to yourself and include all the things you are most proud of and the little details that might get overlooked. Loving yourself and appreciating yourself is the best way to make sure you are taking care of yourself and meeting your highest potential, so don't be shy. Absolutely charm yourself.

1. IN WHAT WAY AM I BEAUTIFUL?

_____
_____
_____
_____
_____
_____

2. IN WHAT WAY AM I LOVING?

_____
_____
_____
_____
_____
_____

3. IN WHAT WAY AM I SPECIAL?

_____
_____
_____
_____
_____
_____
_____

FREE RESPONSE

CRYSTAL CLARITY

It's hard to make the best decisions when you can't see the situation clearly. Sometimes all it takes is a few extra moments to consider the situation from different perspectives. Sometimes we need to stop and gather more information. Whatever it is we need to do to understand the situation, it's important that we try to make it as clear as possible before rushing ahead. In this way we can make our best decisions, rather than recklessly waste opportunity.

1. IN WHAT SITUATION DO I NEED MORE CLARITY?

2. HOW CAN I CLARIFY THE SITUATION?

3. WHAT CAN I DO ONCE I UNDERSTAND THE SITUATION BETTER?

FREE RESPONSE

TRAILBLAZING

In some cases, it's important not to stray from the path (in the woods, for example). Metaphorically, however, it's difficult to innovate unless you try something different. Just because something has worked one way a thousand times before does not mean that it's impossible to find a *better* way of doing things. You will never know unless you try, so the next time you get a brilliant idea that you're too intimidated to try, think about what you stand to gain if you succeed. You could be leading the way to something revolutionary.

1. WHERE IN MY LIFE DO I NEED TO STRAY FROM THE ROUTINE?

___

2. HOW CAN I MAKE MY OWN WAY?

___

3. WHAT CHANGES CAN I BRING?

___

FREE RESPONSE

I AM STRONG

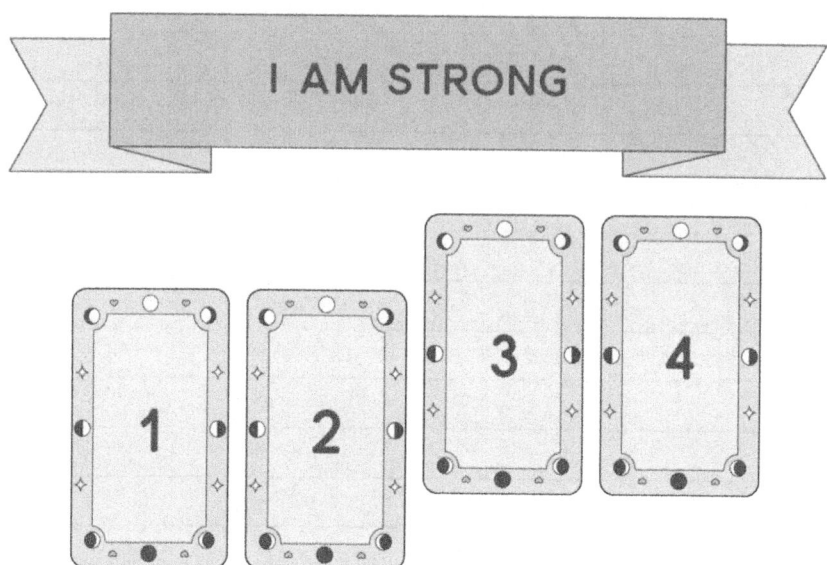

If nothing else, remember one thing: you are strong. You are capable of overcoming so many challenges if you just have faith in yourself. Know that every day you do something challenging, you get a little stronger and you become capable of doing a little more. Keeping this in mind makes you more confident, it makes you braver, and it makes you better. Recognize your strengths and you can do anything.

1. WHAT IS ONE OF MY GREATEST STRENGTHS?

___

2. HOW CAN I APPLY MY STRENGTHS TO MY CURRENT CHALLENGE?

___

3. HOW CAN I MAKE MYSELF STRONGER?

___

4. WHAT CAN I DO WITH MY STRENGTH?

___

FREE RESPONSE

ABOUT THE AUTHOR

Maria Morales was born and raised in California to Lidia and Jorge Morales, two Mexican immigrants who gave her every opportunity they didn't have. Her sister, Ariana, showed her what could be accomplished with those opportunities. Maria served in the U.S. Navy for three years until she was diagnosed with Bipolar Disorder and medically separated. She is now a mental health advocate. She is also the creator of the Pastel Magic Tarot Deck and the owner of Mulberry Moons. She currently resides in Washington with her partner, Eddie, and their two cats and two dogs. Together, they dedicate their lives to the pursuit of continuous self-improvement.

www.mulberrymoons.com

Made in the USA
Middletown, DE
15 December 2019